Untamed

THE WORKBOOK

Copyright © 2023 by GuideGuru Publishing

All rights reserved. No part of this publication may be reproduced, distributed, or transmitted in any form or by any means, including photocopying, recording, or other electronic or mechanical methods, without the prior written permission of the publisher, except in the case of brief quotations embodied in critical reviews and certain other noncommercial uses permitted by copyright law. For permission requests, write to the publisher at the address below.

Disclaimer:

The workbook provides educational insights for personal growth and self-discovery. It is for general educational purposes only, aiming to inspire individuals to embrace their true selves, challenge societal norms, and explore personal growth areas. Readers should exercise personal judgment, respect boundaries, and seek professional advice for specific mental health or personal issues. No specific results are guaranteed, as self-discovery is a unique and ongoing process for each individual. By using this workbook, readers accept the disclaimer, acknowledging their responsibility for any consequences arising from its use.

Thank you for choosing to engage with this book. We hope it helps you build a healthy and loving relationship with your partner.

LESSONS IN THIS WORKBOOK:

1. Unleashing the Wild Within

2. The Power of Unraveling

3. Embracing the Wilderness

4. Unruly Love

5. Living Out Loud

Chapter 1: Unleashing the Wild Within

Lesson 1:

Embrace your true self

Reflect on societal expectations: Take a few minutes to list down the societal expectations that have influenced your life, such as career choices, appearance, or relationships. How have these expectations affected your sense of self? Have they limited your true potential? Write about any instances where you have felt pressured to conform to these expectations and how it made you feel.

Discover your passions and interests: Make a list of activities, hobbies, or interests that genuinely excite and energize you. Write about why these pursuits bring you joy and fulfillment. How can you incorporate more of these activities into your life? Describe how aligning with your true passions can lead to a greater sense of authenticity.

_____
_____
_____
_____
_____
_____
_____
_____
_____
_____
_____
_____
_____
_____
_____
_____
_____
_____
_____
_____
_____
_____
_____

Define your values and beliefs: Reflect on your core values and beliefs. Write about the principles that are important to you and why they resonate with your true self. How can you integrate these values into your daily life? Describe how living in alignment with your values can help you embrace your authentic self and make decisions that reflect who you truly are.

Lesson 2:

Rejecting societal norms.

Questioning societal norms: Choose one societal norm related to gender roles, appearance, or behavior that you would like to challenge. Write about why this norm feels limiting or restrictive to you. How has it influenced your life? Share your thoughts on how breaking free from this norm could lead to personal growth and empowerment.

Redefining your own standards: Reflect on the societal expectations that have shaped your perception of femininity or masculinity. Write about how these expectations have affected your self-image and choices. Now, create a list of qualities or attributes that you personally believe define femininity or masculinity. Describe how embracing these personal definitions can help you create your own path and live authentically.

Celebrating uniqueness: Think about a time when you or someone you know challenged societal norms and embraced their uniqueness. Write about this experience and how it inspired you. Describe how you can celebrate your own uniqueness and encourage others to do the same. How can embracing your individuality contribute to personal fulfillment and a more inclusive society?

Lesson 3:

Embracing discomfort

Identifying your comfort zone: Write about the activities, situations, or behaviors that make you feel comfortable and safe. Reflect on why you tend to stay within these boundaries. Describe any instances where you have felt reluctant to step outside your comfort zone and what held you back.

_____
_____
_____
_____
_____
_____
_____
_____
_____
_____
_____
_____
_____
_____
_____
_____
_____
_____
_____
_____
_____
_____
_____
_____
_____
_____
_____

Stepping into the unknown: Think of a situation or opportunity that feels unfamiliar or challenging to you. Write about the potential benefits and growth opportunities that could arise from embracing this discomfort. Describe the actions you can take to push yourself beyond your comfort zone and how you can overcome any fears or doubts.

_____
_____
_____
_____
_____
_____
_____
_____
_____
_____
_____
_____
_____
_____
_____
_____
_____
_____
_____
_____
_____
_____
_____
_____
_____
_____

Learning from discomfort: Recall a past experience where you felt uncomfortable or faced a significant challenge. Write about the lessons you learned from that experience and how it contributed to your personal growth. Reflect on how you can apply those lessons to future situations that require stepping outside your comfort zone. Share your thoughts on how embracing discomfort can lead to a richer and more fulfilling life.

_____
_____
_____
_____
_____
_____
_____
_____
_____
_____
_____
_____
_____
_____
_____
_____
_____
_____
_____
_____
_____
_____
_____
_____
_____
_____
_____

Chapter 2:
The Power of Unraveling

Lesson 1:

Unraveling societal conditioning

Reflect on a specific belief or behavior you have that you suspect may have been influenced by societal conditioning. Write down how you think societal norms and expectations might have played a role in developing this belief or behavior. Then, brainstorm alternative perspectives or approaches that align more with your authentic self.

Take a few minutes to observe your daily routines and habits. Write down any instances where you notice yourself conforming to societal expectations without questioning them. How could you challenge these norms and add more authenticity to your life?

_____
_____
_____
_____
_____
_____
_____
_____
_____
_____
_____
_____
_____
_____
_____
_____
_____
_____
_____
_____
_____
_____
_____
_____
_____
_____
_____
_____
_____

Write a letter to yourself from the perspective of your authentic self, free from societal conditioning. Describe how this version of you thinks, feels, and behaves differently. Discuss the positive changes you can make by embracing your true self and letting go of societal expectations.

Lesson 2:

Honoring personal boundaries.

Reflect on a recent situation where you felt your personal boundaries were crossed or compromised. Write down how it made you feel and the impact it had on your well-being. Identify the specific boundary that was violated and consider how you could have communicated and enforced that boundary more effectively.

Create a list of your core values and priorities in life. Write a short paragraph explaining why each value or priority is important to you. Then, identify any boundaries that need to be set to align with these values and protect your well-being. Write down specific actions or statements you can use to assert these boundaries in various situations.

Imagine a scenario where you find it difficult to say "no" or enforce your boundaries. Write a dialogue between yourself and the other person, practicing how you would communicate your boundaries assertively and respectfully. Focus on using "I" statements and expressing your needs clearly.

Lesson 3:

Embracing vulnerability.

Reflect on a time when you avoided vulnerability due to fear or discomfort. Write down the specific emotions and thoughts that were holding you back. Then, challenge those fears by writing down the potential positive outcomes and personal growth that could result from embracing vulnerability in that situation.

Make a list of three areas in your life where you tend to strive for perfection or avoid taking risks due to fear of failure or judgment. For each area, write a paragraph describing how embracing vulnerability could enhance your growth, relationships, or overall well-being. Identify specific actions or steps you can take to move towards embracing vulnerability in those areas.

Write a journal entry about a recent experience where you allowed yourself to be vulnerable. Describe the situation, your initial hesitations or fears, and how it felt to open up and embrace vulnerability. Reflect on any positive outcomes or connections that resulted from this experience, and how you can apply this lesson to future situations.

Chapter 3: Embracing the Wilderness

Lesson 1:

Embracing solitude and silence.

Find a quiet and comfortable space where you can be alone with your thoughts. Set a timer for 10 minutes and engage in free-writing. Write down whatever comes to your mind without judgment or censorship. Reflect on the thoughts and feelings that emerge during this solitude, and note any insights or realizations you gained from the experience.

Create a list of activities or practices that you can engage in to intentionally seek solitude and silence. Write down at least five activities that resonate with you, such as taking nature walks, meditating, journaling, or sitting in a peaceful spot. Commit to incorporating one of these activities into your weekly routine and write a brief reflection on how it impacted your state of mind and well-being.

Imagine yourself in a tranquil natural setting, surrounded by solitude and silence. Close your eyes and vividly describe this scene in writing, using sensory details to paint a picture of the environment. Reflect on the emotions and sensations that arise as you immerse yourself in this imagined solitude. Consider how you can bring elements of this experience into your daily life.

Lesson 2:

Connecting with nature

Take a nature walk or find a peaceful spot outdoors. Observe the natural environment around you and choose one element that captures your attention—a flower, a tree, a bird, or any other living being. Write a detailed description of this element, noting its colors, textures, sounds, and movements. Reflect on the interconnectedness of this living being with the larger ecosystem and how it contributes to the beauty and balance of nature.

Create a gratitude journal specifically dedicated to nature. Each day, write down three things you are grateful for in the natural world. These could be experiences, sights, sounds, or even small interactions with animals or plants. Reflect on how these moments of connection with nature make you feel and the positive impact they have on your overall well-being.

Write a letter to a future generation, describing the beauty and wonder of nature as you see it today. Share your hopes and aspirations for the preservation of the natural world and the importance of fostering a deep connection with nature. Express your commitment to taking individual actions that contribute to the well-being of the planet and invite the reader to do the same.

Lesson 3:

Living in the present moment

Set aside 10 minutes each day to engage in reflective writing on the topic of mindfulness. Write about your experiences with being present in the moment and the challenges you face in maintaining mindfulness. Explore strategies or techniques that have helped you cultivate greater presence in your life. Reflect on any changes or shifts you have noticed in your overall well-being as a result of practicing mindfulness.

Create a "Mindful Moments" journal. Throughout the day, pause for a few minutes to fully immerse yourself in an everyday activity or experience. It could be savoring a cup of tea, listening to the sounds of nature, or engaging in a conversation with a loved one. After each mindful moment, write a brief entry in your journal describing the experience and how it felt to be fully present. Reflect on the impact of these moments on your overall sense of contentment and connection.

Choose a photograph or image that represents a significant moment or memory in your life. Reflect on this image and write a detailed description of the scene, the emotions it evokes, and the lessons you learned from that experience. Consider how revisiting this memory can serve as a reminder to be present and fully engage with the richness of life in the present moment.

Chapter 4: Unruly Love

Lesson 1:

Love as liberation

Reflect on your current understanding and beliefs about love. Write down a definition of love that aligns with the concept of liberation and empowerment. Consider how this new definition expands your perspective and challenges any preconceived notions you may have held. Share an example of how embracing love as liberation can positively impact your life and relationships.

Think about a situation or relationship where you have felt limited or constrained by traditional ideas of love. Write a letter to yourself, offering words of encouragement and empowerment. Discuss how you can shift your mindset and actions to embrace love as a liberating force, allowing yourself and others to grow and flourish. Outline specific steps you can take to embody this new understanding of love in that situation or relationship.

Choose a quote or poem that resonates with the idea of love as liberation. Write a response to the quote, explaining how it relates to your personal experiences and the changes you would like to make in your understanding and expression of love. Reflect on the potential impact this shift in perception can have on your well-being and relationships.

Lesson 2:

Love without conditions.

Create a list of five qualities or aspects of yourself that you have previously judged or criticized. Write a compassionate and accepting letter to yourself, acknowledging these perceived flaws and expressing unconditional love and acceptance for them. Reflect on how embracing self-love without conditions can contribute to your personal growth and well-being.

Think about a challenging relationship in your life. Write a letter to the person involved, expressing your desire to cultivate a love without conditions. Share specific examples of how you intend to approach the relationship with acceptance, empathy, and respect, regardless of any perceived shortcomings. Reflect on the potential impact this shift in perspective can have on the dynamics and quality of the relationship.

Write a short story or narrative that illustrates the power and beauty of unconditional love. It could be a fictional tale or a personal anecdote. Focus on the transformative effects of accepting and celebrating the inherent worth of individuals, despite their imperfections. Reflect on the lessons and insights gained from writing this story and consider how you can apply those principles to your own life and relationships.

Lesson 3:

Honoring relationships.

Make a list of the key relationships in your life, such as family, friends, or romantic partners. Write a reflection on each relationship, noting the qualities that make it meaningful and authentic. Identify specific actions or behaviors you can engage in to further honor and nurture those connections. Consider how you can contribute to the mutual respect, support, and growth within each relationship.

Choose a significant relationship from your past that has experienced challenges or conflicts. Write a letter to the person involved, expressing your desire to honor the relationship and work towards healing and growth. Share your reflections on the lessons learned from the difficulties faced and discuss your commitment to cultivating a more meaningful and authentic connection moving forward.

Write a set of guidelines or principles for yourself that reflect your intentions for cultivating meaningful relationships. Include values such as respect, empathy, active listening, and support. Reflect on how practicing these principles can enhance the quality of your relationships and contribute to personal and collective growth. Write a short reflection on the potential challenges you may encounter while implementing these principles and how you can overcome them.

Chapter 5: Living Out Loud

Lesson 1:

Living your truth

Reflect on a time when you felt compelled to hide or suppress an important aspect of yourself. Write down how it made you feel and the impact it had on your well-being and sense of authenticity. Identify one action you can take today to begin living in alignment with your truth and express that aspect of yourself more authentically.

Create a personal manifesto that reflects your values, desires, and dreams. Write down a series of statements that declare your intentions to live your truth unapologetically. Display this manifesto in a place where you can see it daily as a reminder and source of inspiration.

Imagine your ideal life where you are living your truth fully. Write a detailed description of this life, including the activities you engage in, the relationships you have, and the impact you make. Reflect on the steps you can take today to start aligning your current life with this vision, and write down three actionable goals that will bring you closer to living your truth.

Lesson 2:

Taking risks

Write a letter to your future self, reflecting on a bold risk you have been hesitant to take. Describe the potential rewards and growth that could come from taking that risk. Address any fears or doubts you may have, and offer words of encouragement and support to your future self as you navigate the journey.

Make a list of three risks you would like to take in your personal or professional life. Write down the potential benefits of each risk and the specific steps you need to take to prepare for and execute them. Reflect on the lessons you could learn from each risk, regardless of the outcome.

Write a short story or narrative about a fictional character who takes a bold risk and faces failure along the way. Describe the character's emotions, challenges, and eventual growth. Reflect on the lessons you can draw from this story and how you can apply them to your own life as you embrace risks and navigate failure.

Lesson 3:

Embracing creativity

Set a timer for 10 minutes and engage in free-writing. Write without judgment or inhibition, allowing your thoughts and ideas to flow freely. Explore a topic or theme that sparks your curiosity or interest. Reflect on the experience and the insights you gained from tapping into your creativity in this way.

Create a vision board or collage that represents your creative expression. Use images, words, and colors that resonate with you and reflect your unique artistic voice. Write a brief explanation of the symbolism and meaning behind each element on your vision board.

Write a letter to your inner critic, the voice that often judges or inhibits your creativity. Engage in a dialogue with this inner critic, challenging its limitations and offering counterarguments that encourage self-expression and creative exploration. Reflect on the power dynamics between your creativity and your inner critic, and how you can cultivate a more supportive and nurturing relationship with your creative self.